Why Battle Frontline

People watching is one of the most frustrating and experiences. Human nature is frustrating because that's what makes us so amusing. My home town c   , East Sussex is no different from anywhere else. Sometimes it's the individual, at other times it is groups of people and all too often it is those in a position of authority that betray their flawed humanity. We have a choice. We can rant and rave at their stupidity, or we can just laugh at their antics (and our own). I prefer the latter - it makes life so much more enjoyable! I hope you find these few pages interesting, perhaps insightful, but most of all I hope it makes you smile, chuckle, or even have a great big belly laugh.

On 13th October 2015 I plucked-up the courage to email the local newspaper to offer my services. I enclosed a few short articles, including what turned-out to be a controversial poem, about dog poo (reproduced later in this publication) and was passed-on to the Commissioning Editor, who responded a few weeks later:

"Your idea sounds like a fine idea. I would need to pin you down to a regular time slot to help our page planning - could I suggest the fourth Friday of the month? There needs to be a word count of approx 450 words. plus a picture of some sort.

Of course, I'm sure you understand you're doing this for the glamorous lifestyle that accompanies such accolade, not any form of financial remuneration (just to be clear!).

If this sounds suitable, perhaps we could aim for Friday November 27 edition, in which case I would need copy by Friday 20."

And so it happened. I became the 'Battle Chronicler', writing a monthly column of 450 words called "Frontline News" . A star was born, albeit an unpaid one.

What follows is the result of 2 years of snooping around the town to get under its skin and help the reader understand what it is really like to be a resident of Battle.

David Horne

Contents

1. Battel Bonfire Boyes – November 2015 bonfire celebrations
2. Lightening the Winter Blues – singing in the face of Battle
3. Battle of the Coffee Shops – why so many?
4. Let us Go Over to the Other Side – religious observance and Network Rail
5. Yoga can be Served in a Variety of Flavours – how do you take yours?
6. Good Friday Marbles – the religious versus the secular
7. Battle for Europe – Brexit and Battle
8. Sedlescombe's got Talent – but Battle has enthusiasm
9. The Reluctant Mole-catcher – a dying rural profession
10. Battle of the Scarecrows – the annual scarecrow fest
11. A Stitch in Time – A modern 'Bayeux'
12. Beware the Twin-striped Parking Python – preying on motorists
13. Normans Win with Last Shot of Match – Senlac re-enacted
14. The Dark of Battle – Battle at night
15. Forgive us our Trespassers – encounter with an irate farmer
16. Blood-letting in Battle – First Blood
17. Blood-letting in Battle – Mines a Pint
18. The Pirate King – preparing to do Battle
19. The Pirate King – the audition

20. Doorstep Revelations – all sorts can knock on your door

21. A Pocket-full of Rye – Battle's twin-sister in focus

22. Dancing with the Common People – jiving with ordinary Battle folk

23. Signs of the Times – at war with the English language

24. Where is the Bexhill Link Road? – lost road to the seaside

25. Don't do Nothing, when Doggies Do – ode to a dog turd

26. Waiting to be Processed – thoughts from a doctor's surgery

27. Frontline News Extra – Battle 2066

Battel Bonfire Boyes

Context:

During the months of October and November each year groups of fancy-dressed, flaming-torch-bearing marchers come together in towns across East Sussex to celebrate Guy Fawkes Night. In my experience most people have fireworks or attend bonfires on or near November 5th each year, but no-where celebrates it quite like they do in East Sussex. One of the best bonfire societies is Battel Bonfire Boyes, who raise significant sums of money for charity and put on one of the most popular shows in the county. We regularly attend the Battle event, which still manages to blow my mind each year. Battle has the distinction of parading the oldest Guy Fawkes in the world in a wooden tumbrel. Some 20,000 people gather in the High Street to watch several hundred marchers parade to the beat of drums and the ear-splitting crack of bangers thrown into open topped beer barrels.

Column:

Mayhem comes to the streets of Battle each year, in November. This year we were accompanied by three guests as we made our way into town to observe this November ritual. Having had a beer before coming out, my bladder was demanding I visit the public toilets by the Market Place. As I picked my way between Henry VIII, the Archbishop of Canterbury and Captain Mainwaring, I seemed to move into a parallel universe where such juxtaposed characters were the norm – like a Lewis Caroll adventure. I would not have batted an eyelid had the urinals either side of me been occupied by Tweedledum and Tweedledee.

The different bonfire societies of East Sussex have widely different dress codes. Some are dressed in red and black horizontal striped jumpers, slightly reminiscent of

Dennis the Menace and Minnie the Minx. Others prefer period dress - English kings and queens, soldiers from World War One or grenadiers from the Zulu Wars. Yet another genre is the black-clad, top hatted ghoul or tightly-corseted, overly-rouged 'lasciviant'. Most groups are accompanied by a band of rhythmic drummers, many of whom were already beating themselves into a frenzy of excitement.

The High Street, was worlds apart from the genteel tourist town of the daylight hours. However, the absence of traffic during such Battle events is always welcome, enabling us to walk freely and drink in the atmosphere.

As the evening progressed, some several thousands of merry-makers from all over East Sussex and beyond, crowded onto The Green to witness the spectacle of the torch-bearing participants marching the length of the town, accompanied by the drum bands and beer barrels on wheels. These last were like modern day Roaring Megs, into which bangers were periodically dropped, with the resultant bang amplified to an ear shattering explosion.

At the head of the procession was wheeled the oldest 'Guy' in the world. A caricature Guy Fawkes being driven in a tumbrel to his ceremonial execution. The culmination of the ceremony involved the participants throwing their flaming torches onto a large bonfire and the burning of a modern-day effigy of Mr Fawkes. The firework display that followed was almost tranquilising in its effect, compared to the frenzied swarm of humanity that preceded it.

One might reasonably assume that the original Guy Fawkes was burned at the stake for his treasonous behaviour. In fact he was condemned to death by being hung, drawn and quartered - probably a much less acceptable way of celebrating these days. In reality Guy Fakes was never executed, since he cheated the hangman's noose by falling off the scaffold and breaking his neck. Let's just stick to bonfires shall we?

November 2015

******

Lightening the Winter Blues

Context:

By the time we get to December, Battle is starting to feel the icy grip of winter. However, Christmas is just around the corner, providing the opportunity for at least two musical groups to break-out into song. Battle Light Opera Group put on four performances over a November weekend at The Battle Memorial Halls - anything from Gilbert and Sullivan to Steven Sondheim. The whole production is carried off superbly by the talent and enthusiasm of local amateurs.

Battle Community Singers are likewise keen amateurs, who at Christmas time are like as not to be found singing carols beneath the massive Christmas Tree that adorns The Green, outside the gates of Battle Abbey.

Column:

The midwinter solstice celebrations (otherwise known as Christmas) are regarded by many as a way to offset the short, dark, cold, windy and wet days of December. From November through to February we welcome any opportunity to lift our spirits with music, song, dance and humour.

Battle has its own exponents of singing away the recent winter blues, including Battle Light Opera Group (BLOG) and Battle Community Singers. Both groups provide the ordinary public with a chance to become involved in performing, regardless of their talent. I've been looking for an outlet for my dubious talent, ever since I moved to Battle 3 years ago, and thankfully both groups took me in.

The recent Mikado production by BLOG was probably the best since Drowsy Chaperone 2 years ago and the only one since then not to incorporate my "dubious talent". Ah well. They did let me paint the scenery (not the glorious backcloth picture of Fujiyama, but the white emulsion undercoat on the side flats

- which were later overpainted with light blue!). As ever, the star of the show was enthusiasm. Talent was there as well, but 'am-dram' has to be mostly about enthusiastic community involvement, be it on-stage, backstage, front-of-house, the audience, or just people painting the undercoat on the light blue side flats.

I have to confess that watching a well performed and enthusiastic BLOG production can be even more enjoyable than being in it. Certainly much easier. This time the show was a fast moving update to Gilbert and Sullivan's original, being a bazaar mix of Japanese history and geography, but with English characterisation. Even the light blue side flats were beautifully undercoated.

Battle Community Singers is a quite different approach to community involvement. For the last 6 weeks, twenty or so of us have been singing our hearts out to master a collection of 'Christmas Favourites' such as White Christmas, Guadete and Come all Ye Faithful. The 30 minute performance on 10th December at Battle Gala Late Night Shopping, hopefully brought a few rays of sunshine into the frozen winter hearts of pre-Christmas shoppers.

A few shoppers paused to listen to three community choirs brave enough to sing under Battle's swaying Noble Fir, as the bracing winter wind clinked the wassailing balls and threatened to fuse the Christmas tree lights. But it was our moment in the limelight and no-one was going to take it away from us.

It could well be that the performances of both these wonderful local singing groups will stimulate a few more 'Battle hardened' souls to have a go themselves and reap the benefits of community involvement. Failing this, why not make a date to patronise future performances.

As in that well-known Japanese saying "Even undercoat painters have a role - when it comes to lightening the winter blues".

December 2015

******

Battle of the Coffee Shops

Context:

When I first came to Battle I couldn't help but notice what a busy shopping centre it is for a town with only about 6,000 residents. It had a green-grocer, a butcher, a news-agent and a super-market – all of the things you might expect of a town, that is little more than a village. What sets it apart is the number of hairdressers, boutiques, gift shops and cafes. None of the above are of a great deal of use to me personally since I have virtually no hair, I am male, I have Yorkshire heritage and if I'm thirsty I go home for a free cuppa.

Fortunately not everyone is like me, otherwise Battle traders would quickly go out of business. Further, the population of Battle swells rapidly in the day time as large numbers of tourist cars, coaches and rail passengers descend upon the town to visit Battle Abbey. Unlike me, they do need cafes for refreshments and many of the other outlets which are always prepared to assist them with a bit of retail therapy.

I suspect few of them make use of the large number of hairdressers – but that's a story for another day. My Frontline News column for January focussed on the number of coffee shops, particularly because the Today programme had just run a piece about the large number of coffee shops in Totnes – over 20 it seemed. So I decided to see if Battle came anywhere near it.

Column:

When I first moved to Battle a few years ago, I accompanied my wife to the station and was struck by the number of coffee outlets that there are in the town. At the station I realised a man was even selling coffee and snacks there (our former mayor in fact). I approached him and said "How many coffee shops do you think there are in Battle?" After a bit of ritual sucking of teeth he said "Half a dozen?" "No", I said triumphantly. "There are at least 20 by my reckoning." A little later, with my wife suitably waived off at the station, I departed, with the poor man still working out where I got my 20 from.

Like any investigator worth his salt, out came the notebook and pen and off I went to count them all. I decided I could include all of the pubs and restaurants, as they too provide coffee. I even counted the Esso garage that sells coffee in paper cups and the lady selling refreshments in the auction rooms that were open that day. Well why not?

I had already counted six by the time I'd reached the High Street and decided to cross The Green and write down the names of coffee parlours on that side of the road. As I recorded them in my book, the door of one of the coffee shops shot open and a Spanish looking gentleman, called out to me. "Hey wadda ya writin in ya book? My car is only parked there for a minute!" "Oh I'm just recording how many coffee providers there are in Battle. How many do you think?" I added, to take the sting out of the situation.

He was by now all smiles. "I don't know – perhaps twelve?" "No." I replied, with a note of authority in my voice. "At least 20". At this he became less coherent and I suspect was muttering something along the lines of "No wonder I don't-a make-a much-a money!" Had I played my cards right I might have got a free coffee out of him.

As I moved up the High Street the number of hot beverage outlets continued to rise and passed twelve as I reached Costa Coffee. It seemed ironic that a Spaniard ran the English Tearoom adjacent to Battle Abbey, yet Costa Coffee appeared to be run by spotty English teenagers. By the time I had made the Market Place I had counted a grand total of 25 coffee sellers littering the main road through Battle.

This may in part explain why the Saxons lost in 1066, if there were as many back then. Too many coffees on the way to Senlac Hill would have required them to momentarily turn their backs on the Norman's, for a leak. A fatal error. The rest, as they say, is history.

January 2016

******

Let us Go Over to the Other Side

Context:

Throughout my life I have had periods when I had an interest in, or a need for organised religion. One such period was when I moved to Battle shortly before my wife and I decided to get married. Doubtless wanting a church wedding had some bearing on this, rekindling my desire to share in collective worship with my fellow man.

The Church is not a particularly trendy establishment these days, with many people able to take or leave it. However, in centuries past the right to worship how, when and where you chose was jealously guarded. Wars, persecution and sectarianism over religion are hopefully things that are firmly in our past, but if anything should get in the way of our religious freedoms we are quick to defend our rights.

Column:

Battle is a town divided. It is divided by Network Rail, or more particularly the barrier on Marley Lane level crossing. The greatest sufferers must be those poor souls who 'live on the wrong side of the tracks' and are prevented from getting into the town. But it has an impact upon all of us looking to move freely about the district.

On Sunday 31st January I was on my way to the Emmanuel Centre, to share in worship with the rest of the congregation. I am not a regular worshipper, but I had a desire to attend this new church and enjoy a bit of quiet contemplation.

Alas I suspect the congregation was a little depleted on Sunday. Throughout history many have tried to prevent Christians from taking part in acts of collective worship. The 1st Century Romans come to mind; Protestant and Catholic factions of the church itself, during the Reformation; and recently the actions of organisations such as ISIS, in the Middle East. However, this Sunday a new threat to Christian worship surfaced – Network Rail.

As I approached the level crossing at 10.23 am I could see that the red lights were flashing and the barrier was down. My heart sank, only to be lifted when the Hastings-bound train passed through within 10 seconds. I waited expectantly for the barrier to rise, but no such consolation arrived. Instead myself and a growing queue of cars sat patiently by, waiting for something to happen.

You could almost hear the groans from the other cars, when a minute's delay turned to 5. I turned on the radio, only to hear that Terry Wogan had passed-away that morning. I wondered what joke he might have cracked at the expense of Network Rail.

By the time 10 minutes had elapsed a number of people were out of their cars. Some were craning their necks to see what was happening, others were gesticulating in animated fashion to fellow sufferers, but most of us just sat tapping our thumbs on the steering wheel.

By the time 15 minutes had passed, even the passengers from the Hastings bound train had arrived at the crossing. Ironically they too were unable to cross the very railway line that had promised to speed them home, or perhaps to the Emmanuel Centre? A large proportion of the queueing cars had decided to change their travel plans and were now going through that most forlorn of car manoeuvres, the 10-point-traffic-jam-turn.

Eventually I also cracked, deciding that like Job I too was being tested by The Almighty. All hope of quiet contemplation had been shattered. Nonetheless I was resolved to make the most of my loss, by writing to both Network Rail and our local MP. Having duly despatched my emails, my righteousness restored, I thought I might as well make some amends for my non-attendance at church by opening the Bible. I opened it up at Mark 4:12 verse 35

'That day when evening came, he said to his disciples, "Let us go over to the other side". '

I hope he had more luck crossing the Sea of Galilee than I did crossing Marley Lane level crossing!

February 2016

******

Yoga can be Served in a Variety of Flavours

Context:

Since my early 50's I have been increasingly aware of aches and pains, especially around the joints. This is an understandable result of gathering senescence. However, not being a fan of throwing in the towel or accepting my lot, I have spent my later years in search of the fountain of youth – or at least a close facsimile of it. Yoga appears to come closest, allowing me to retain a modicum of mobility when all about are loosing theirs.

So one of the first things we had to look for on moving to Battle, was a yoga class. However, yoga comes in all sorts of forms, with no two classes the same.

Column:

My first encounter with Yoga in Battle was on a chilly and slightly misty October evening. The venue an unlikely looking bungalow on Marley Lane, which through the gathering mist looked like the set of a Hammer House of Horrors movie. There were no signs of life, other than 2 cars parked on the drive and a single electric lamp illuminating the front door.

With more than a little misgiving, Frances and I knocked on the door. It was eventually opened by a small, black-leotarded lady, with a slightly disjointed, perhaps Transylvanian accent.

"Hello. Haf you come to ze Yoga class? Ve started at 6.30 but you are most velcome to join us."

After a brief interrogation regarding our previous yoga experience, we eventually found ourselves in a warm, dimly lit room whose floor was covered in a thick pile carpet. As my eyes grew accustomed to the gloom, I could see three other bodies arranged on the floor, demonstrating terribly contorted and painful positions. At this my mood darkened, until I realised they were in the process of adopting a yoga position.

I took my place next to a very large gentleman. I soon realised that his enthusiasm far outstripped his yogic capabilities, when at one point we were instructed to adopt whatever vertical pose we wished. With surprising agility my neighbour attempted a headstand. This greatly vexed our now highly animated instructor, who reprimanded him severely for adopting an unsafe posture. I had to agree. I could easily have ended up as a smear next to him, on the thick pile carpet.

For the next hour my neighbour did manage to keep his enthusiasm in check. However, when our host announced that we would finish with yogic nose blowing, we made hurried excuses and departed. The whole experience was more akin to that of a mystical, quasi-religious Indian sect, then the simple weekly flexibility work-out that we really wanted.

A few weeks later we chanced upon another class, which was being held at Battle Memorial Halls. As we entered the main hall I immediately realised that this was what I wanted, especially when Debbie, our Australian instructor, greeted us all in a cheery 'girl-next-door' manner.

The session started with a sitting posture and finished lying down, eyes closed in a darkened room – both of which I am quite adept at. In between I confess there was quite a lot of stretching, holding of positions and the inevitable grunting. However, some two years later we are still attending the class. Encouragingly, 25% of us are ageing males, desperately struggling to match our more flexible female counterparts.

In fairness some will prefer their yoga flavoured with saffron and other eastern spices, but I'll take mine natural and served from 'down-under' every time!

March 2016

******

Good Friday Marbles

Context:

Easter, particularly Good Friday, is a time of year when the secular and religious overlap. Of course one can observe both aspects of British life. The Christian community celebrates the event which launched a new religion some 2000 years ago – the crucifixion of Jesus of Nazareth. The new religion probably absorbed the significant calendar activities of previous religions.

Easter is set as the Sunday following the first full moon after the spring equinox. In which case I suppose you would call it a 'moveable feast', unlike Christmas which is always on 25th December. Like Christmas, Easter celebrations involve a mix of traditional activities, commercial opportunism and Christian worship.

In Battle, a growing local tradition is the Good Friday Marbles Match when local teams of 5 form to fight for the title of champions. They also compete in fancy dress, some of which can be quite bazaar and probably handicap their performance of the former.

In the end there is nothing to prevent both religious and secular groups and individuals getting involved either in the marbles or the religious observance. In 2016 I was pleased to witness both.

Column:

To some Easter means chocolate eggs and having a good time. To others it marks the death of Jesus, probably on Friday 3rd April AD33. However, for many there is room for both. Good Friday can therefore be a day of celebration, of sad reflection, or both.

So it was that on Good Friday this year I decided to walk into Battle on a sunny, if rather fresh spring morning to observe the town and some of its people. My first port of call was Battle Baptist

Church. As I sat amongst the gathering throng I considered the rough cross, at the front. It seemed strange that this instrument of execution and torture should form the centre-piece. Strange, but powerful, on this of all days.

As the service commenced, dominated by the singing of Easter songs, I was nearly brought to tears. It was as if I were attending one of many family funerals, scattered over the years. In reality I was. The occasion was oddly cathartic, but left me me emotionally drained. I confess I left before its conclusion, yet uplifted.

As I returned to the spring sunshine, a group of ladies dressed as boxes of Easter eggs, went before me. As we made our way down the High Street, joined by others in fancy-dress it was evident that I had effectively moved from the atmosphere of a funeral, to that of a wake.

Arrayed round The Green were enough trestle tables to equip a wall-paperer's convention. Each offered tempting foods, games or artefacts designed to entice the Easter celebrant. The smooth tones of a crooner filled the air, mixing with the smell of burgers and everywhere was bright colours. Probably half of those attending, sported unusual dress. Nursery rhyme characters, a bridal entourage and even Captain Mainwaring and his home guard, mingled with an air of conviviality. Bizarrely, the components of a full English Breakfast sat exchanging views on one of the benches.

Central to it all were the marbles' boards, overseen by top-hatted umpires intent on ensuring due propriety between contesting teams. The competition bore none of the intensity I recall from my playground years. Back in the 1960s the stakes were high, with winner takes all. Instead members of each team politely took it in turns to propel a large 'glass-alley' at a collection of small white marbles, gathered at the far end of a board. Whenever a marble was struck, a ripple of applause and cheering broke out.

This was essentially a sport for the committed participant. So as a mere spectator I quietly melted away and returned to everyday life. Perhaps as most spectators to the events in Jerusalem did two thousand years ago?

April 2016

******

Battle for Europe?

Context:

Brexit has been a contentious issue for the last 5 years and will probably continue to be so for many more to come. In a democracy we are all entitled to our individual opinions on such matters, hopefully with all concerned expressing those opinions with due respect for the opposing point of view and without rancour.

The difference of opinion over Brexit began well before the 2016 referendum. In this column I felt I should lend my voice to the debate, even if the only opinions I was going to influence were the 'half-dozen' or so readers of it.

Battle has a unique history of European conflict, but at the same time it is a Mecca for visitors from our European neighbours, who bring economic benefits and sometimes a little conflict of their own to our local community.

Column:

The other day I walked through Battle and noted a number of children disembarking from a coach parked at The Green. They were all from French schools, based on my tenuous grasp of the French tongue. Evidently they had come to rub our Saxon noses in the fact that their forefathers slaughtered ours here 950 years ago. Come October they will be back in even larger numbers to re-enact the whole event as usual. I wonder if there is a reciprocal arrangement at Agincourt?

Recently I watched a 'legends' football match on TV, between England and Germany. It was to celebrate 50 years since we beat them in the World Cup. Some of us still recall the event. Not surprisingly the German team took it all very seriously, fielding a squad of ex-professionals, whilst the English squad contained a large number of comics. The English thought it was going to be a light hearted re-enactment of the 1966 thriller. The German's had not surprisingly come to spoil the party. Who can blame them? In front of 30,000 baying English fans they put the English to the sword 2-7. It didn't really matter

Every 10 years, old soldiers gather in Flanders or Normandy to commemorate one or other of the two World Wars. Not a glorious re-enactment this, but a sharing of sadness for past aggression. War is not a pretty thing and it does matter.

Wars, be they in 1066 or the Twentieth Century, are caused by a small number of power-seeking individuals misleading a whole nation into fighting a neighbouring one. This, rather than economic benefits, was the initiator of what we now call the EU. The thinking was that countries that have close trading relations are less likely to go to war. Unfortunately the British government of the time did not share the same ideology. It was only once our empire had crumbled around us and we found ourselves in a sad economic state, that we belatedly asked if we could join in the European project.

Over the last 40 odd years the UK has thrived economically and socially. As we have become more integrated into Europe, so the likelihood of us ever going to war with our European neighbours has diminished. Unfortunately the politics of greed and jingoism are threatening to reverse this process through Brexit.

What a pity it took over 900 years for European countries to work together in close political harmony. Had the EU existed in 1066 there might never have been 10 or 20,000 dead on Senlac Hill, let alone the millions involved in European Wars since.

As our children move freely around Europe, working and studying with fellow Europeans, so they will learn to respect and celebrate their differences. In Battle of all places, those who can still recall the misery of wars, or who heard of it first hand from their parents, should discourage divisions based on nationalism, and put their energy into improving, not obstructing, the European dream.

May 2016

******

Sedlescombe's Got Talent

Context:

Four years into our Battle adventure, we decided to add further to our list of social opportunities. A friend of ours runs the Battle Community Singers which appealed to us since it involved singing with a printed sheet of words in front of us, rather than memorising them. I particularly enjoyed my celebrity status as one of a minority of male singers in the group, almost all of whom were ladies of accumulated years.

Our leader regularly arranged for us to perform in front of an audience, including relatives, residents of an old people's home, or singing carols under the Christmas tree at The Green. However, on this occasion we were going to compete with others for a significant financial prize. Further, we would be playing away from home at the nearby village of Sedlescombe.

Column:

A few weeks ago Euro madness came to our television sets. Nothing to do with Brexit or football, but the Eurovision Song Contest. This year Australia were the special guests and nearly caused a major upset by carrying the trophy off down-under. Fortunately for the European Dream they only made second place.

About the same time, a parallel competition was taking place in Sedlescombe. Several local acts queued up for the opportunity of carrying off this prestigious award and the £100 prize money. However, the 'Australians' in this scaled-down version of Eurovision were Battle Community Singers, including myself.

Doubtless a number of Sedlescombe residents grumbled in their beer when these outsiders were announced. Numerically, on grounds of cumulative age and on pure enthusiasm we should have won hands down, however, this was to be a competition based upon talent, so 'Battle' lines were drawn, as we dreamed of doing an 'Australia'.

First out of the blocks was Charles rapping the curls out of many a greying perm, followed by Macarthur matching him with energetic dance moves and the removal of outer clothing - which made the Vicar look distinctly uncomfortable.

Our compare served-up some well-practiced clichés to engage the audience, including "I've not got my Friday teeth in" with each slip of the tongue and "The bar is still open", when business looked a bit slack. My favourite was "Sausage Rolls are going half price". Alas for me, I missed out in the rush that ensued. They like a bargain in Sedlescombe. The excitement was ratcheted-up still further during the interval, when the winners of the raffle were announced. This brought all sorts of gasps from the lucky few, including one apoplectic lady who carried off a whole basket of bananas!

After the break, our troop gathered backstage in expectant silence, like latter day tommies waiting to go over the top. Suddenly we were on, as 13 sets of squeaking hips and knee joints formed up on a stage just big enough for 12. Somehow we crooned and jived our way through a medley of African songs, the meaning of whose words were doubtless lost on our audience.

Our performance completed, the audience politely rippled their applause, as we tentatively crocodiled our way down the steep stage steps. Surprisingly we achieved this without ropes or casualties and gratefully returned to our seats, ready to enjoy the last two acts.

It was perhaps fortunate, or more likely by design, that the last two contestants performed when they did. Such was their calibre, that had they performed first all the other acts would have gone home before the interval.

As the panel announced and justified their choices of winners, the results were hardly in doubt. It seems Sedlescombe does have Talent after all. Call it sour grapes, but personally I think talent is over-rated. Bring on Battle's got Enthusiasm – we're certs to win that one.

June 2016

******

The Reluctant Mole-catcher

Context:

The best way to discover the joys of the High Weald countryside that surrounds Battle, is to pull on hiking boots and waterproofs and walk the local footpaths. There is no shortage of these ancient route-ways, which take the walker through quaint villages, ancient woodland and grazing pasture.

You can meet some fascinating people on your travels and get into brief but instructive conversation with them. Life stories give the most interesting insight into the local area, including farmers, shop-keepers and publicans.

On this occasion we had the good fortune to bump into a professional whose occupation may be seen by some as a little grizzly, but it is always good to hear the other person's point of view, which in the countryside is often very practical.

Column:

Whilst out on a day's walk along the footpaths around Battle, Frances and I paused to check the route. A grey-haired figure crouched over his quad bike, came speeding across the field and pulled up nearby.

"Good morning" He bid us in a cheery voice.

"Are you the farmer" Frances asked.

"No" He replied, "I'm just the mole-catcher."

At this he proceeded to tell us about what he was doing, laying traps in the ground to catch the 'gentlemen in velvet'. We asked if we might watch him at his work, of which he was only too willing to oblige.

"I don't like killing things" He said. Which was an interesting confidence for a mole-catcher to share with a couple of complete strangers. "I just do it for the farmer, because he's always been good to me".

"I once reluctantly agreed to trap a mole for an elderly lady, who had mole hills on the lawn. When I came back I found one caught by its foot In my trap. I felt so sorry for the poor thing, I let it go"

Doubtless mole-catching is a solitary business, so he must have felt that a pair of eager listeners were heaven-sent and proceeded to give us a treatise on moles and their catching.

Evidently they live in a system of underground tunnels, with the spoil being pushed onto the surface as mole-hills. The mole hills make the growing grass dirty, something the discerning cows apparently turn their noses up at and thereby impacting the hay crop's value. Further, it seems the mole hills become as hard as concrete in the summer, causing damage to hay-cutting blades.

All this he explained as he went about his business of finding the position of a tunnel, using a prod. Once located, a divot of earth was removed and "voila", there was Mr Mole's motorway. Next he took a pair of small stainless-steel traps from an old ice-cream container and placed them back-to-back blocking the run. The unsuspecting mole's fate was effectively sealed, whatever direction he approached from. Next our man carefully shovelled loose earth around the traps and returned the divot. A white stick marked the position of the traps, for when he returned in a day or two.

How enlightening it was to learn first-hand about the business of mole-catching, an occupation that has existed for centuries. Traditional practice was for dead moles to be hung in gruesome collections on a nearby branch. Not-so our reluctant mole-catcher, his preference was to bury them in their runs. In the words of Ewan McColl "Through all their lives they dug a grave …."

Although moles are found throughout Britain, for some reason they are not found in Ireland. It would appear that snakes were not the only things banished by Saint Patrick.

July 2016

******

Battle of the Scarecrows

Context:

Every year Battle is home to a well patronised scarecrow competition, with entries exhibited all around the town. Each year has a different theme to keep entrants on their toes and provide the rest of us with a fresh new chapter in the Battle Scarecrow book. I recall that when we moved to Battle in 2012 there were lots of Olympians and Para-olympians on display.

2016 has seen a ramping-up of 1066 activities, celebrating the 950th anniversary of The Battle of Hastings. So it comes as no surprise that Battle Scarecrows had to adopt the same theme.

It is always fun to see what take the residents and Battle businesses have on a given topic. The Battle of Hastings provided lots of opportunities for them to flex their little grey cells.

Column:

A stranger to Battle, arriving here after dark, could be forgiven for thinking the town is a centre for violent behaviour. The fact of the matter is that until recently the streets of Battle were awash with heavily armed ne'r-do-wells skulking in dark alleys and open spaces. The Green in particular attracted large numbers of these miscreants.

Fortunately the streets have now been cleared of 1066 scarecrows and we can go about our law abiding business once again. I had the good fortune to encounter these men of war during daylight hours, inspecting their fearsome weapons and burnished armour at close quarters, as I considered who to vote for.

I started off my tour of the gathered armies at The Market Place, where I quickly despatched a soldier dressed in Saxon-looking attire. Somehow he had acquired a helmet from the Knights Templar a century or so later.

Next I admired King Harold himself outside the Battle Museum. Despite his convincing Saxon moustache I had to penalise him for trying to pass off Edith

Swan-Neck as his wife. His 'official' wife was Edith of Mercia, so I had to disqualify him on a technicality.

Making my way down the high street as I ticked them off one by one. I was particularly attracted to one character in a long coat outside Shire Country Clothing. Alas he was not a scarecrow, but a tailors dummy. Nice coat though.

At the Market Place I encountered a range of zombie clergy and nuns, and a Norman archer with a solar panel in his heel (whilst the Norman's were chucking arrows, are we really to believe that the Saxons were lobbing bits of 21st Century electrical goods in the other direction?). There was William The Bastard riding a flowerpot horse and at Barrocloughs Opticians and there was even Harold Godwinson on horseback, observing Halley's Comet through industrial spectacles.

Battle Books had made a token effort. Oops - pardon the pun! But history does not record Harry Potter being present at the Battle of Hastings. Sorry, wrong Harold! I also had to disqualify Alan Hunting Associates, because at the time of my visit there was a very large corvid in front of it. So technically it was a failed scarecrow.

At the time of writing I am blissfully unaware of the outcome of the competition but to my mind there could only be one winner - Battle Floral and Horticultural Society. This scarecrow was neither a Saxon nor a Norman, but the husband of Betty of Battle. This modern-day character had a Saxon eyeball complete with arrow, on the end of his garden fork. It reprised the story of Richard III being discovered under a car park in Leicester and raised the very topical question as to where exactly did England's most famous battle actually take place?

August 2016

******

A Stitch in Time

Context:

Once again the focus on The Battle of Hastings was to provide rich pickings for the Frontline News column. The Bayeux Tapestry was an iconic piece of art work commissioned by the victor, William of Normandy's half brother – Bishop Odo. It was a kind of cartoon strip stitched into a long thin roll of cloth.

Most tapestries were designed to cover an entire wall and reduce the draughtiness of the castles that the rich and powerful occupied at the time. At a mere 20 inches in height, Odo may have just employed it as a conventional under-door draught excluder. However, it is more likely that it made for a good bedtime read, with the added benefit of providing plenty of exercise as he walked its 230 foot length before bed.

Not wanting to waste a good idea, one of Battle's more creative residents came up with the idea of creating a tapestry to commemorate how Battle has changed since 1066. The Battle Tapestry was to be the work of local people (whereas Odo employed Kentish weavers to make his). Residents and visitors alike were encouraged to pop down to the council offices at The Almonry, where under expert instruction they would add a few stitches of their own.

Column:

The celebrations of 950 years of Norman rule are gathering pace. Before you know it the town will once again be swamped with 'Normans', who will as always vanquish the gathered Saxon hordes. I'm talking about the 1066 re-enactment of course and not some forthcoming Apocalypse. Violent death is a terrible thing, as is the forced occupation of another country, but the events of 1066 are so far removed from modern day life that it all passes off as just a bit of fun.

Similarly, the Bayeaux Tapestry was little more than a gory retelling of the story and a celebration of Norman dominance over the Saxons. So it was refreshing to come across a new version of the famous 'carpet on the wall', being stitched here in Battle. Refreshing because the 'Battle Tapestry' depicts the post-Battle of Hastings events that shaped our lovely town from 950 years ago.

Along with my visiting sister and her two sons, I toddled off to the Almonry to see if I could add a few stitches to this historic piece of textile. My wife and her mother had tried to muscle in on the act once before, only to be rebuffed by an occupying army of Japanese tourists. When we returned a couple of weeks later, we found that most of the 'easy' bits had been done – perhaps by our oriental contributors.

"Would you mind returning next week and we'll have something easy for you to do then?"

This time we were in better luck, although the younger of my two nephews was adamant that at the tender age of 16 he had had quite enough of needle-work at school. Over the ensuing hour my sister, her 22 year old son and I applied ourselves to the tapestry with much the same concentration as the Bayeaux Tapestry stitchers of old must have done. My sister, probably because of her gender, was given a curved line to stitch, whilst we mere menfolk were charged with stitching just a bit of straight line. I have to say I thought I did remarkably well. I took a photograph of my work, in order to help me find my contribution when it is displayed upon its completion later this year.

I suspect this 'peoples tapestry', contributed-to by several hundred members of the public, is not a repeat of the process used by the Canterbury-based seamstresses back in Norman times. At 230 feet long it would probably have taken the whole of the last 950 years to complete. In fact it is believed to have had a more recent contribution. Close inspection of the famous arrow in Harold's eye is revealed to have been added during the 18th Century. Photo-shopping it seems is not a modern day technique.

With this is in mind, my photograph of my original stitch-work will be compared with the finished product when it is exhibited. Woe-betide if I should find anyone has edited my contribution!

September 2016

******

Beware the Twin-striped Parking Python

Context:

Living in a tourist town has its drawbacks – traffic and attendant road parking problems. However, in my experience it is not tourist traffic that is the main problem, since I am fairly confident that most of them either park in the Rother DC car parks, or the car park at Battle Abbey - where many of them are bound.

Battle is also something of a route centre and a good place for through traffic to stop-off at for a quickie purchase. These do not want to spend time walking from the car park for a loaf of bread, nor do they want a £1 surcharge on it , by way of purchasing a ticket. Likewise, I suspect a significant number of locals park at the roadside.

In 2016 matters came to a head, especially when the town became wrapped in the coils of the twin-striped parking python.

Column:

A large snake is to be found lurking in the gutters of Battle. It is highly visible, having two distinct parallel yellow stripes along its back. Pedestrians need have no fear of this lurking reptile as it skulks between the drains and the litter of most of Battles town centre roads.

It has been observable for many years on much of the High Street, Upper Lake and Lower Lake. However, the species is apparently extending its range, now found snaking its way up Calbec Hill, along North Trade Road and down Marley Lane. It even occupies the gutters of most of the minor roads of Battle. It is everywhere!

"How does it live, what does it feed on?" I hear you ask. Well, whilst pedestrians need have no fear of it, motorists beware. Not those who keep moving, since it is a relatively slow predator. In fact you can probably pull up next to one for a few minutes and suffer no ill effects. However, it will probably bite if you risk any longer than this! And its bite can be terrible indeed.

Until recently most people avoided the Twin Striped Parking Python, as it is commonly known, by leaving their car in one of the snake-free reserves to be found around the town. Of course entry to these comes at a price. Alternatively you can park beyond its range and walk into town.

Some clever folk have sought out havens of their own closer to the town centre. At least one shop-keeper I know has coughed up and joined English Heritage, so that he can keep his horseless carriage safely tethered in their snake-free coral all day long. Another acquaintance of mine has noticed a circadian rhythm operates on the High Street, where between 6.30pm and 7pm, serpent-free islands miraculously appear, giving him time to nip into the chippy for his chicken and mushroom pie with chips. I have my own special place, but I have no intention of sharing its whereabouts with anybody reading this.

Interestingly enough, I have noticed that a number of residents appear to have developed an immunity to the snake. For example one such person is now happy to leave their four wheeled friend parked outside an estate agents on Mount Street all day and every day. Have they developed some kind of snake repellent, or has our predatory beast lost its venomous bite? Time will tell.

In the meantime, cars continue to herd through the town centre, fearing to pause for too long, vainly searching for a safe place to rest for an hour or two, because who knows when the creature will next strike and who will its victim be? You perhaps?

October 2016

Footnote:

For several years after, motorist quickly learned that they could park with impunity on double yellow lines, since Rother District Council was loath to employ a traffic warden to enforce the law. This led to open defiance of the law, a dangerous precedent to allow in any civil society. Fortunately a change in local politics has seen a change in local authority control. Perhaps when driverless cars eventually become common-place, they will drop their passengers off at the shops, returning to pick them up again a few minutes later. But then scores of driverless cars circulating around Battle may bring its own traffic issues!

******

Normans Win With Last Shot of Match
(Saxons 0 – Normans 1)

Context:

Twelve months had passed since the first Frontline News column appeared, by which time the annual invasion of the town by Normans and Saxons alike was due. Each year English Heritage puts on a re-enactment of The Battle of Hastings, but to celebrate the 950th anniversary they were to push the boat out a bit, with over 1,000 armoured Saxon and Norman footsoldiers, scores of horses and some serious weaponry.

You are never far from 1066 in Battle - the defining year of the town's history. By now I was starting to feel a bit of a celebrity, even though I had no idea if anyone even read my column. Still, as a member of the local press I thought I would flex my media muscles a little and ask English Heritage for a couple of free tickets for the Battle of Hastings re-enactment. Imagine my delight when they duly arrived and Frances and I were able to waive them at the gate as we walked boldly in!

Column:

On Sunday 16th October I joined the masses descending upon Battle Abbey for the 950th Anniversary re-enactment. On Friday night I had observed numerous individuals outside the pubs around town, dressed appropriately. There was even a group of native-born Normans staggering between The Bull and The Kings Head, singing some incomprehensible and ribald song in French.

On entering Battle Abbey grounds we made our way to the battlefield, where the main action was to be held. As I wandered through the Saxon encampment it was apparent how seriously they were taking the whole re-enactment thing. Not an i-pad or mobile phone in sight. All were dressed in simple cloth and ate bread, cheese and apples of a millennium earlier. By contrast many of their 21st Century visitors consumed large quantities of fish and chips from Battle 'chippy'.

As I wandered around the encampment I was struck by the tenseness of the atmosphere. Some of the Saxons happily engaged with the spectators, explaining finer points of 11th century weaponry, but the majority of the menfolk were more withdrawn, awaiting the imminent clash of arms. I cornered two young soldiers clad in chain-mail and asked them if they felt the adrenalin yet.

"Just starting" one replied with a wry smile "once we start to gather and the chanting begins, then it really kicks in."

When I asked them about the fighting, you could see the excitement in their eyes.

"I took three groin hits in this morning's fight and I almost 'lost it'" One said, referring to his temper rather than any threat to his reproductive capacity.

"The arrows are not pointed but they still leave a nasty bruise on the arms or legs if you get hit." Said the other. "But you get a real sense of what it must have been like, particularly facing a man with a lance on a charging horse. You just don't see the lance coming."

The Norman encampment was much the same, but all the conversation was in French. A group of Norman soldiers knelt in prayer as a priest delivered a blessing and then exhorted them to smash English skulls. Sounds like the EU and Brexit is not a new phenomenon.

As they marched off there came a cry from one - in English "Today we go to die at Battle Abbey"

Whilst another shouted rather incongruously. "Vive Napoleon".

The battle that followed was a well-choreographed stage show, which seemed almost tame by comparison with the very real emotions I had witnessed from the participants beforehand. At the end, as Edith Swan-neck searched the battlefield for her dead king, a belligerent voice shouted "It never happened!"

950 years on, you could almost hear 10,000 lost souls turning in their graves.

November 2016

******

The Dark of Battle

Context:

Anyone moving from London to the countryside for the first time will be shocked by their first night-time experience. As a species we are so dependent upon our vision that when it is removed, albeit temporarily, we are suddenly very vulnerable.

Ex-city dwellers are understandably fearful of being mugged, beaten-up or murdered in any dark place. Local people don't seem to have the same problem, probably because there is not enough business for muggers in the countryside. After all muggers are unlikely to even see a prospective victim on a country lane on 364 nights of the year!

Mugging aside, when it comes to walking local roads, darkness and poor adaptation to it carries real consequences for the poorly illuminated pedestrian.

Column:

It is flattering to find that this column is not only reporting the news, but making it also. In October I drew attention to the "Twin Striped Parking Python". Low and behold the topic dominated 4 pages of the 8th December issue. I'm hoping this month's column will likewise stimulate serious discussion.

Having moved to Battle four years ago from East London I was immediately struck by the existence of darkness. Real darkness. This is a double-edged sword, with the joy of seeing the Milky Way tempered by a fear of being run over on Netherfield Hill, when returning home in the 'wee hours' from a social gathering in the town.

One of my earliest observations of Battle is that it appears to be inhabited by hordes of 'cat-burglars', spies and the man from the 'Milk Tray' adverts of the 1960s. I draw this conclusion from driving after dark, when I frequently catch one or two of these fleeting black-clad figures in my headlights. They are the lucky ones, as it seems almost inevitable that one day one of them will see their luck run out and they can expect a permanent rendezvous with an even better known black clad figure – brandishing a scythe.

During my Black Battle induction period I quickly discovered the simple expedient of wearing a 'hi-viz' vest and carrying a torch at night time. This has served me well up until now, although the lack of a pedestrian footway along Netherfield Road and Netherfield Hill means even brightly clad pedestrians such as I, risk life and limb during every excursion into town – day or night.

Our darkly clad night time walkers appear to labour under the illogical assumption that if they can see a car coming, then surely the driver of the car can see them also. This erroneous assumption is effectively the reverse of an ostrich putting his head in the sand. Even more surprising is the probability that most of these black clad pedestrians are themselves drivers and will have had a close encounter with one of their pedestrian-selves on numerous occasions.

Perhaps older residents are too set in their ways to change their walking habits and wear something white, or carry a torch. However, wherever possible we have to do our level best to encourage the younger generation to make themselves more 'hi-viz'. This said, anyone who has shared a house with a teenager knows how belligerent they can be. How do you get a 'Goth' to wear something white? One simple solution might be to buy them a black leather jacket emblazoned with a flashing skull and crossbones on the back. After all, to my knowledge no member of the Battle Chapter of The Hells Angels has ever been the pedestrian victim of a night-time road traffic accident.

December 2016

******

Forgive us our Trespasses

Context:

We have been walking the footpaths of Battle and the High Weald for many years, rarely falling foul of dogs, horses, cows, overgrown paths or fellow humans. But then all things must come to an end.

Most walkers, especially the few that we meet in the blessed isolation of the High Weald, don't want to go anywhere other than the dedicated public right of way. Trespassing is not a desirable option since the public rights of way are usually the easiest routes to follow. Overgrown paths, poor signage and poorly maintained stiles are the main cause of deviation from the well-worn tracks of the area.

In this instance we came unstuck because in some of the local woodland walkers are permitted freedom of access eg. Forestry Commission, Woodland Trust, National Trust. So be extra careful here!

To avoid walker–landowner conflict, we carry a 1:25,000 map at all times and report any access problems to East Sussex County Council. On the other-hand landowners should ensure waymarks, footpath signs, gates and stiles are well maintained. A sign indicating the correct route is going to be far more beneficial to all concerned, than one stating the opposite.

Column:

"How did you get over my stock fence?" were his opening words of welcome, when he spotted us.

They were not meant to be cordial. The farmer was obviously more than a little annoyed, that two middle-aged walkers had managed to breach his high security fence, designed to keep out the masses of deer in the local woods. Well we had. There was no denying it.

It all began as a pleasant circular walk round Battle. As the day progressed, we realised time was getting short, so on entering some woodland we decided to take a shortcut using a compass. This works alright in open moorland, but less well in woodland.

Puffing and grunting, we eventually made it to the edge of the wood, only to have a taste of what it must be like for Syrian refugees trying to escape across Europe. Before us stood an 8-foot high fence.

The thick brambles made further woodland walking nigh impossible. So more in hope than expectation we struck out alongside the fence, looking for a possible opening in our iron curtain. Spotting a place where a badger must have forced its way under the wire, I somehow was able to push head and shoulders through the self-same gap. Within a couple of minutes, coats, bags and a very muddy looking Frances had joined me.

Our euphoria soon passed. The only way out was going to be along a farm track to the main road. As we rounded a corner, before us was a man in a large digger. I expected a dog, or even a shotgun, but thought a large digger was a bit over the top for dealing with trespassers.

As we approached, the digger driver emerged and posed his question "How did you get over my stock fence?"

I could see it was time to eat some humble pie "We were lost in the woods and found a place where a badger must have squeezed under".

This seemed to placate him a bit. Perhaps it reassured him that at least we hadn't cut a hole through it. For some reason I could hear the theme tune to The Great Escape, playing in my subconscious. Perhaps he thought we had jumped over using a motor-bike? But not even Steve McQueen had managed that!

"Where have you parked?" He asked.

"Nowhere" I replied, "we live in Battle".

His whole demeanour suddenly changed. A bit of pleasant chit-chat about the weather and a final apology from us and we were on our way. Amazing!

I wonder, does being a local trump the sins of trespass? Most walkers do prefer to follow footpaths, but of course there will always be the occasional rotten apple who has the temerity to wriggle under an 8-foot high deer-fence.

Please - Forgive us our Trespasses.

January 2017

******

Blood Letting in Battle – First Blood

Context:

Being limited to 500 or 600 words for a newspaper column is excellent discipline for anyone who is overfond of his own 'voice'. It makes you look long and hard at your writing. Nonetheless, there are times when you might feel more words are needed. I found a way around this by running a story over two separate months. After-all Charles Dickens started writing his novels in serialized form. His approach was a paradigm shift which changed literary publishing. I was just a little late to the party.

The first two-parter addressed my initial experience of giving blood, at the tender age of 60. I had always been a bit fearful of the idea of losing blood under any circumstances. Perhaps by the age of 60 I felt I had had a good innings and just gave myself up to the needle. However, I like to think it was the ambiance of the Battle Memorial Halls and the calmness that retiring to the High Weald had given to me, which finally drove me into the arms of the waiting medical profession.

Column:

I am the proud possessor of a badge which says I have given blood 10 times. My first donation was a few years ago at Battle Memorial Halls:

Boldly I march into the main hall, where a waiting male nurse stands ready to greet the latest raw recruit.

"Welcome" says the nurse, "Name and date of birth". To which I give the appropriate response. "Have you given blood before?" He continues. "No" I reply, like a teenager being interrogated about his virginity.

He presents me with a clipboard, to which is attached a paper full of questions.

"Could you please fill in the answers to the questions on this side, but leave the other, as we will fill this in ourselves"

As I work through it I am pleasantly surprised to realise that there is actually a good chance that I will know all the answers. It is also evident that 'No' is the preferred answer to most of them, and as the column of 'No' ticks grows my confidence rises.

Then the trick question appears - "For women only: Have you ever .....?" Now I am stymied. What do I put for the answer? After long agonising, I realise that "No" is actually the correct answer, as being a man I am technically incapable of whatever a woman may or may not have done. Duly fortified I tick the 'No' box and continue.

The sheet completed, I hand it to the nurse at the desk, with 100% of answers ticked 'No'. I confidently assume that my passage through to the next stage of blood-giving is a formality. However, as he looks down the list of questions he comes to the 'woman only' questions and pauses.

"You are not supposed to answer the woman only questions" he says, peering over his glasses.

"Oops!" I retort. Appropriately admonished he gives me a leaflet which explains the whole process I am volunteering for and indicates I should read it before being called by yet another nurse.

Several minutes later I report for further questioning. The nurse reads through each question, apparently satisfied with my nice uninterrupted column of 'No' answers. Then she pauses and I know what is coming.

"You answered the 'woman only' questions. Why?" She asks with almost Teutonic directness. I can almost see the monocle falling from her eye.

I respond with a shrug "Is idiot blood unacceptable?" At which she throws me a dagger.

"It is just that answering the 'women only' ones suggests that you didn't read the questions. We need to be sure you did!"

I humbly apologise and promise to do better next time. Having narrowly passed the suitability checks, I am instructed to return to the waiting area in anticipation of the main event – the 'blood-letting' itself! *(To be continued)*

February 2017

******

Blood Letting in Battle – Mine's a Pint

Context:

This is part two of my first two-part column. No-one seemed to mind me spreading my column over 2 months. Either that, or no one noticed. I didn't know how many readers I had, if any, since the newspaper never bother to give me any sort of feedback or guidance, either from readers or from the editorial staff.

I started to wonder if I just wrote out the Lord's Prayer, would it matter in the least? Would anyone notice? Doubtless if I wrote something offensive or objectionable I would get to know soon enough.

I am reminded of how poorly managed some local newspapers can be. Back in the 1970s a friend of mine was paid to write a sporting column for a paper in Derby, but lost interest. Despite not filing any copy, they continued to pay him for several months afterwards. He didn't seem to mind in the least.

Column:

My first donation was a few years ago at Battle Memorial Halls. This involved an initial series of questions, including two 'women only' ones. It won't surprise regular readers that I committed the cardinal sin of answering these, which doubtless convinced the nursing staff that they were dealing with a total idiot:

Having narrowly passed the initial suitability checks, I am instructed to return to the waiting area before being directed to one of the 'blood extraction' seats. I am given an advice sheet and a large red rectangle is stuck on the back of my seat. This is to tell people that it is my first time. I also suspect it is to identify those idiots who are unsure what gender they are! I fear the red rectangle is a coded instruction to staff to "give his head a good slap whenever you pass by".

After lots of fiddling about with tubes and bags I am connected up to the apparatus.

As I relax back in the seat I realise that music is playing in the background. As I listen I am surprised to hear the strains of Norman Greenbaum belting out that well known 1969 hit, "Spirit in the Sky". As I drift off, blood slowly dripping from my left arm, I listen to Norman's words:

> "When I die and they lay me to rest
> Gonna go to the place that's the best".

What kind of twisted mind chose that track?! Oh well, the tune's a good one. After 10 or 15 minutes of the recommended fist clenching and buttock squeezing, a nurse takes the red rectangle from the back of the chair and gives it to me. I'm to carry it with me so that they can keep a close eye on the new boy.

As I join the other 'drained' clients propping up the bar I discover the real reason why I am carrying the red rectangle. The 'bar tender' advises me I can only have orange squash to drink. It seems hot drinks are not available to new boys.

So there I sit like a recalcitrant teenager sitting with his soft drink on the steps of the pub. However, I get my own back by eating a second packet of custard creams!

After 10 minutes I am discharged and wend my slightly light-headed way back home.

I reflect on the entire experience as I walk. I wonder if they all broke down laughing once I had gone.

"What an idiot!" "Answered the women only questions!"

I ponder whether they consigned my hard given blood sample to the bin marked "Idiot Blood". Nonetheless I am proud of the fact that I have finally done my bit for human-kind and am a 'Blood Virgin' no longer.

March 2017

******

The Pirate King - Preparing to do Battle

Context:

This was the second of my two-parters. My piece about giving blood appeared to have gone down well. Or at least no-one had complained about it. I was therefore hopeful that I might be able to do it again.

Retirement to Battle has been kind to me. However, there are instances where advancing years can take their toll. As a chorus regular for Battle Light Opera Group I was starting to get ideas above my station – I fancied being a principle, the focus of attention.

Make-up and lighting can work wonders in live theatre, making Widow Twanky look positively radiant and turning a boy of 13 into a wizened old man of 80. However, the audition has none of these 'cheats' to fall back on. Perhaps a good dose of talent would help, but if you fall short on both counts you are really up against it.

Column:

An audition can go one of two ways. You can give of your best, the panel are gushing in their appreciation and you are given the part. Alternatively - you don't, they don't and you are not. It is all about how those three negatives play out.

So it was, as I prepared for my audition for the part of 'The Pirate King' in Battle Light Opera Group's May 4th - 6th production of Gilbert and Sullivan's 'Pirates of Penzance'. No longer would I be a mere spear carrier. No I was going to be a principle, with his face and biography printed on the program for all to admire.

The Pirate King part was described as "baritone, athletic, handsome, with a playing age of 40." Baritone – fine. Athletic and handsome - hmmm? 40 plus - substantially so! Whilst excesses of the other three attributes were likely to be beneficial, advancing years were definitely not.

It is at moments like these that a confident member of the male gender realises why maturing women spend hours on their make-up, colouring their hair or turning to surgical enhancement. Not to do so is to walk around with a large badge saying "Old fart – not to be taken seriously".

As I stared into the bathroom mirror I could see a face returning my gaze that was becoming more prune-like every day. Then I considered my facial hair. Ten minutes of razor work left me with a neat little goatee. Giving me something between rough pirate and 19th Century nobility. Perfect, with one caveat – my beard was grey.

The solution was obvious, colour. Searching the bathroom cabinet my eye alighted upon what looked like a felt tip pen. Taking the object down, I unscrewed the top, allowing me to draw out a long black brush – mascara. I had the solution (in both senses of the word). If this stuff works on eye lashes, why not on a beard? I'd just need a bit more. Well most of a tube, as it turned out.

The transformation was immediate. 20 years came tumbling off my face. Looking back at me from the mirror was myself in 1996. Astonishing! I had discovered the secret of eternal youth and it came from a small magic bottle, a deep well that I could draw upon as often as I liked. What devious creatures these women can be. Their illusion of youth represents the greatest physical transformation since Lazarus.

With my newfound youth I felt ready to strut my stuff. Fortified with confidence I would sweep all before me. I even tried unbuttoning my shirt to the navel, to encapsulate the devil may care demeanour of a Pirate King. Then I thought better of it and settled for the allure of a single carelessly undone button. Audition? Bring it on! *(to be continued)*

April 2017

******

The Pirate King – The Audition

Context:

This was part two of my second attempt a serializing one of my Battle Chronicler stories. My physical transformation preparations complete I was ready to audition for a role written for a slightly younger man. All I had to do was overcome the second obstacle – talent, or the lack of it.

I hadn't actually considered that others might have the temerity to audition for 'my' part. Further, they might even employ devious tactics to further their own ambitions, such as social standing, fire alarms, speeding cars and 'innocently' proffered chewy toffees.

Column:

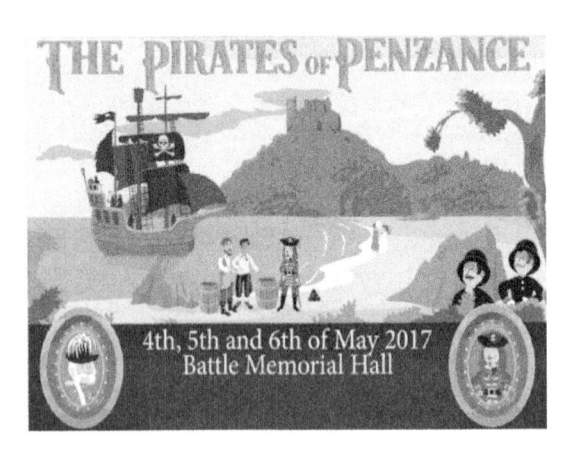

To win the role of The Pirate King at the recent Battle Light Opera Group (BLOG) production I had to overcome the obstacle of auditioning for a part intended for a man 20 years my junior.

Eager to impress I arrive 20 minutes early and help the chairman prepare the hall. As we set out the chairs he breaks out into a rendition of "I am a Pirate King". My song!

I look at this 42 year old and my heart sinks. Before my eyes my photograph and biography are being magically erased from the programme, with a younger alternative being 'photo-shopped' in its place.

There are no fewer than 5 of us up for The Pirate King. Besides the relatively youthful chairman, there are 3 fifty-something candidates and this sixty two year old. The odds are lengthening.

The auditions begin immediately and as each hopeful finishes, rapturous applause fills the room. As I rise to deliver my audition piece, the adrenalin racing through my veins - a fire alarm starts ringing and we all troop out into the street. After 30 minutes of shuffling about in the December cold, the director makes the announcement that we will continue the auditions at Watlington Village Hall.

Having no car, I hitch a lift with one of the other prospective Pirate Kings, the local vet. We are late and he is obviously keen to make up lost time. His urgency and speed at the wheel must have been honed over many years of emergency dashes to assist with the breach birth of a calf. I'm sure this is all designed to undermine my audition – his wife even offers me a chewy toffee – but I am not fooled by that obvious ploy!

On entering the village hall, I am immediately called upon to deliver my rendition of "The Pirate King". I decide to keep it simple and just sing as though I am in the shower – lots of volume and with no attention to the pianist.

Perhaps not the most polished performance of the Gilbert and Sullivan classic, but with a force that guarantees even the deafest person on the back row will hear every word of it. As I finish, I'm sure I notice the director relaxing his hold on some loose papers on the table top. As ever the applause is rapturous.

I sit down, the whole world spinning with me at its epicentre. Thirty years of practice in showers and baths; venting forth during solo car journeys to distant parts of the UK, not to mention to fields full of rather shocked looking cows, have finally come to fulfilment. I am and always will be 'The Pirate King' - whatever the outcome.

As it happens I was not successful - the local vet got the part – pure piracy!

May 2017

Footnote:

Perhaps I should have added a wig. After-all, limited talent is easily outshone by the glare off a balding pate.

******

Doorstep Revelations

Context:

I suspect that at one time people were always rolling-up on your doorstep trying to pedal some service, item or belief. As a child I recall a man calling and offering to sharpen knives with a grinding-wheel attached to his bike. Likewise, I can also recall going door-to-door collecting for Christian Aid as a teenager, in a rather dodgy area of Rotherham and nearly getting beaten up and on one occasion set-upon by a large Alsatian.

Door-knocking is far less common nowadays, with the telephone or cyberspace utilised instead. Perhaps we are more suspicious than in the 'olden days'. I certainly am. However, I don't normally object to sharing religious or political opinions on the doorstep, unless of course I am watching The Cup Final. So when two ladies approached me in my front garden I was happy give them a minute or two of my time.

Column:

I was busy putting my potted tomato plants in my front garden greenhouse, when two ladies approached me.

When the older of the two ladies asked me "Are you the man of the house"

I confess I answered rather suspiciously "I am he – why?"

I confess my suspicious nature derives from being sold some scallops by a mobile fishmonger a few years ago. They were very nice, but not really my cup of tea and expensive to boot.

Unsurprisingly it transpired that they were Jehovah's Witnesses come to share their beliefs. Unlike many people, I quite like to engage in theological discussions on my doorstep. It seemed only polite to give these two members of our local community the opportunity of discussing something of importance to them. For a while at least.

The older lady pressed on, whilst her younger 'novice' stood back, a knowing smile on her face. I suppose they could have been con women, with one keeping my attention, whilst the other cased the joint for alarms and cameras, but I didn't think so.

"We are looking at the Book of Revelations at present"

"Well that's just someone's fantasy." I interjected – perhaps rather crushingly. I then proceeded to explain my customised approach to faith and spirituality.

Spotting an opening she dived in "Oh you believe in God and Creation then?"

"Well" I answered cautiously, "I have been interested in the Environment for as long as I can remember".

Now she was up to speed and started to discourse on her pet subject. However, my interest was starting to wane and the tomato plants were starting to weigh heavy in my arms. As I awaited an opportunity to close the discussion, my mind and eyes started to wander. You notice the strangest of things at these times. The younger 'novice' was wearing a light brown coat, but she appeared to have a large gravy stain on the front. All I could think about was how it got there. Perhaps it was the result of a doorstep altercation with one of my less accommodating neighbours. Whatever the reason, it indicated I should get back to my tomatoes.

So it was that I jumped in and excusing my rudeness, cited my wilting pot plants as the reason to move on. Inevitably the older lady smiled and asked if she could give me a leaflet. Having achieved this modest success, the two of them bid me good day and headed next door. It was only then that I noticed my trouser flies were at half-mast. Doubtless the smiling novice had been as observant about my state of undress as I had been about her gravy stain.

That day it seemed that the saintly John was not the only person to have experienced a Revelation.

June 2017

******

A Pocket-full of Rye

Context:

Rye could be described as a 'sister-town' to Battle. They have much in common, including ancient timber-framed houses, tourism and a rail station. Both are representative of the rural nature of Rother District Council, which is dominated by the relative metropolis of Bexhill-on-Sea.

Every now and then I love to walk the cobbled streets of Rye, especially early in the morning when the town is just waking-up and the tourists have yet to disturb its tranquillity.

I am particularly attached to Rye for another reason. It is where the River Rother finds its way into the sea at Rye Bay. One of the Rother's tributaries, the Brede has its headwaters at the bottom of my garden. Rain falling on my garden will eventually find its way to Rye.

The piece is very reflective and points-out how life can have a certain symmetry. I was born close to the Yorkshire Rother, so it is apt that the latter end of my days should be spent next to its East Sussex counterpart.

For the above reasons I decided that this particular story had a place in my monthly column about Battle and as-ever no-one objected to its inclusion.

Column:

We arrive at Rye with almost an hour to spare before Frances has her orthodontic appointment. Rye is a beautiful little town, often heaving with tourists. However it is even better on a sunny July morning at 10am. Today a gentle breeze drifts across the town from the direction of Dungeness nuclear power station.

Whilst Frances is 'under the knife', I decide to explore. As the town slowly awakens, it is like watching a flower unfold in the morning sun. Shopkeepers are putting out their wares, some carefully but others noisily, as they bustle about their business preparing for the inevitable footfall of tourist customers.

An ancient but dapperly be-hatted decorator is laying out his tools in preparation for yet another day's work. How many times has he gone through this same routine over his extensive working life? Rye exudes tradition and traditional values from its every pore.

Cobbled streets draw me uphill towards the church which sits at the summit, in a position dominating the Rye skyline and visible for miles around. I wonder at the folly of those who choose to buy houses on such cobbled streets. Do they sleep at night, as car tyres rumble noisily by?

As I make my way towards Rye Castle, overlooking the harbour, my attention is drawn towards another more recent artefact of war - Rye war memorial. As in thousands of other villages and towns all over Britain, it bears the names of local servicemen who fell in battle, in both of the major conflicts of the Twentieth Century. Poignantly, additional names have been inscribed on it, marking the deaths of further victims - this time in the Iraq and Gulfs wars. Will it never end?

I am suddenly drawn back into the Twenty-first Century by my vibrating mobile phone. It is Frances, who has evidently survived the dentist's chair. We agree to meet at the castle.

Rye is one of those sensible towns well provided with toilets. I find some nearby. Alas for anyone of advancing years and any degree of infirmity, I discover that the step up to the urinal is so high that I suspect they may shortly need to erect a further memorial - to those of Rye who 'fell-in-toilet'.

As I await the dentally reconstructed Frances, I gaze across the geologically recent flatness of Dungeness and the frequently changed course of the East Sussex Rother. This has to be where I will breathe my last. Born amongst the now defunct coal fields of South Yorkshire on the banks of one Rother, the circle of life demands that I expire close to the banks of another - overlooking a forest of wind turbines and a nuclear power station - the successors to the coal power of my youth.

July 2017

******

Dancing with the Common People

Context:

Back in Battle the summer months burst with excitement as various festivals and events take place. Once again Battel Bonfire Boys take centre stage, erecting a large marquee on the Recreation Ground where local groups are able to showcase their musical talents and where the young, and the not so young, can 'let their hair down'.

Although Battle does have a significant older population, the younger generation are by no means excluded. The town has excellent schools – primary and secondary; it has an impressive play area at the Recreation Ground - with a skate park and football pitches and it is not too far from the urban delights of Hastings.

In case you are just visiting the town for a few hours and wonder what it is like to live here, I can say that after close to a decade in residence, I confess that I like Battle and am proud to be one of its ' Common People'.

Column:

As Glastonbury celebrates its penultimate day of music, we decide to go along to Battle's own budget version - at the Recreation Ground, where Battel Bonfire Boyes have set up a large marquee.

There are no queues and the entry price is a mere £10 each. The down side is that I am fitted with a luminous green wrist bracelet and feel like a sexagenarian ASBO.

Looking around I assess my fellow rockers. Most are in their 30s and 40s. Most of the men-folk are dressed in the obligatory tee-shirts and jeans, many sporting shaven heads. Generally the women have gone to much greater lengths to look their best, some sporting off-the-shoulder outfits which show off a variety of discreet rose, bird and heart tattoos bedecking their shoulders, necks and lumbar regions.

"Take my hand, together we can rock and roll" is the cue for a number of forty-something mothers to go into an impromptu line dancing sequence of dance steps that they doubtless honed 30 years earlier, as teenagers on the dance floor.

Having drained my pint of bitter purchased at the bar, I decide to head for one of the blue Portaloos in search of bladder relief. I confess I have another more illicit reason to hide there - I have smuggled a can of Speckled Hen in with me. It weighs heavily in my coat pocket and I wish to go un-noticed as I transfer its liquid contents to my beer glass.

As I close the door behind me, I pull the offending can from out of my pocket and tug on the ring-pull. Dance induced froth explodes from within. Five minutes later the can's contents occupy the glass, but it has a two inch head on it. A knock comes at the door, so I quickly exit clutching my frothy pint and re-join the masses, where my guilty froth is the more easily hidden from view.

By this time the main act, is blasting out the decibels, as a couple of hundred extra bodies pile into the marquee, dancing to the music of Pulp. The words of Jarvis Cocker are particularly appropriate to the event "I want to live like common people" as we all sway in time to the music. We are the common people.

On the way out I feel the shape of an upturned empty can of Speckled Hen in my pocket. Passing a well-placed litter bin I have the cheek to drop it in, relieved that now there is no evidence of my illicit contraband - except for a small beery smelling damp patch in my coat pocket. Now I not only "live like the common people", I smell like one too.

August 2017

******

Signs of the Times

Context:

The 'Battle Chronicler' in me was tiring of delivering Frontline News. I daresay people get pleasure out of watching goldfish in a bowl, but without some kind of feedback (fish-food in their case) they will soon expire. I was that goldfish and I needed sustenance.

Nearly two years of unpaid, unheralded work for the local paper was starting to wear thin and it was time to pull the rug out from under the project. Ironically I had at least enough articles to see me through to the New Year, when I would go in search of new writing projects.

It was August and other than tourist activity, nothing much seemed to catch my attention in the town. So I took a walk in town looking for inspiration and noticed a few interesting signs put up by retailers.

Feeling a tad mischievous I decided to attempt a satirical piece aimed at the English language, its ambiguities and its misuse.

Column:

It is a pleasant sunny August day. This is a perfect opportunity to seek out a story in Battle during the busy tourist months.

As I enter House of Cards I notice that there is a chalk board outside listing all the good reasons why I should give my patronage to their business. At the bottom of the board is written "Air Conditioning" – very attractive on a hot summer's day. Alas the shop door is propped open, negating the effect of any air conditioning unit that may be running. I suspect it is busted. However it starts me wondering if there is a story to be found spotting ambiguities in the signs up and down Battle High Street.

First on my list is Battle Deli. They have a mass of chalkboards detailing their latest offerings, but I am most taken by "Rear seating". This suggests sitting as we know it is a recent innovation. Perhaps previous seating was only for those prepared to do a headstand on it?

Next is William Hill. The front of the shop is bedecked with "shop closed" posters, although I am drawn to one of their strap lines which says "When the fun stops, stop". I assume it did, so they did – hence the closure.

Further up the road I notice the sign above the recently closed Battle Book Shop heralds the return of "White Sails". It is fitting that a sign in the window says "Sale", but is it exclusive to white goods?

Crossing the road I come to Battle Café and Fish Bar where yet another chalkboard announces "OAP Fish and Chips". I generally prefer my fish to be less world weary. Perhaps with all the over-fishing of North Sea fish stocks, all the younger ones have been taken.

Walking to the bottom of the High Street I am sad to find that Mrs Burton has encountered marital problems, with her café now renamed "Burtons". Her next-door neighbour has also undergone a rebrand, with the Pilgrim's Rest café being renamed "The Nook". I'm not sure of the rationale behind the change, but I suppose it is preferable to "The Cranny".

Not to be outdone, "The Lounge" is reopening as "The Lavender Tea Room". The painters have been in and the whole façade radiates a glorious lavender glow. Hopefully they will offer less flowery flavours of tea also.

Well August is the silly season when it comes to finding a good news story – even in sleepy Battle. At least when looking for signs of local news I'm never going to be far from home and a nice, free cuppa. Chin-chin.

September 2017

Alas this article heralded the end of Frontline News, when a number of Battle traders and their cronies complained that it was "vile and disgusting". But that is a whole Battle news story in its own right.

******

Where is The Bexhill Link Road?

Context:

One day in August I was driving to Hastings when I saw road signs at the Bannatynne's Spa roundabout (see photo below). I was struck that despite the building of the new link road, the road signs still directed drivers seeking Bexhill, down Battle Road. I decided to put myself in the shoes of someone wanting to go to Bexhill along this brand-new multi-million pound new highway. As I drove I found myself being directed around the houses and eventually abandoned outside ESK. I decided to continue in the assumption that an out-of-town driver would eventually be set onto the correct road. It never happened. I would not be surprised if several years later the signs are unchanged. Perhaps you would like to follow in the footsteps, or tyre-tracks, of Darren and Sharon and see for yourself? I filed the story early as I was going on holiday, before the previous 'Signs of the Times' piece hit the fan.

Column:

When Bexhill Link Road was finished, Rother District Council had a competition to name it. Combe Valley Way was selected. My suggestion of 'Billy the Bastards Bexhill Bypass' fell on deaf ears. One of the key reasons for building the £125 million link road was to improve matters for the road travelling public. However, anyone approaching 1066 Country from the north will find precious little road sign evidence to suggest it was ever built. You would have thought a few quid more, spent on signposting, would have been justified.

Put yourself in the shoes of Darren and Sharon driving down from Romford for a day out in Bexhill:

"Shazza and me, we set off for Bexhill to visit mi Nan an 'ave a bit of a paddle in the sea.

Lenny next door said "make sure you use yer sat-nav"

But I just laughed and said "Don't be daft - we'll just follow the road signs"

The M25 and Dartford Tunnel were pretty quiet. We turned off down the A21 following the signs for Hastings and Bexhill - nice road, but it turned into a bit of a cart-track south of Tunbridge Wells.

At a place called John's Cross we came to a roundabout.

Shazza said. "Look Dazza, a sign to Bexhill and Battle".

A good straight road, but a bit bumpy, until we got to Battle.

We stopped and asked an old geezer wiv a funny accent and a bit of straw between his teeth "Oi mate, which way to Bexhill?"

He sez. "You'll be wanting the Bexhill Link Road. At the roundabout with the horse on it, turn left through the town".

"Good on yer mate!" I shouted and we drove through Battle 'til we got to Bannatyne's Spa.

The road sign here pointed straight over and down Battle Road. Well we didn't see any more signs for Bexhill. Not one. We went past Asda and right down into Hastings. Nothin'. We followed the road past ESK, round a loop and back past ESK again, heading back up the A21 towards London.

Shazza said. "Oi Dazza, why we going back t'wards London?"

I just said "Don't you worry girl, the council know what they're doing. Just keep your eyes peeled for signs to Bexhill."

Well we drove all the way up the A21 past Sainsbury's and through the countryside, 'til we found a road sign to Bexhill off to the left. Blow me, if we weren't back at John's Cross again!

I said "Shazza – they spend all that money on a new bloody road and then they keep it secret from us. Well they can stick it!"

And we drove back to Romford."

October 2017

******

Don't do Nothing - when Doggies Do

Context:

Wanting to try something a little different, for the November issue, but still present my Frontline News column as a public service voice, I decided to offer the following humorous poem to draw attention the issue of dog mess in public places.

Column:

Urban parks are blighted by the unwanted by-products of the canine counter-culture. I was a dog owner for several years, but like most readers of this column, never in the confines of a metropolitan environment. Dogs have to be exercised and they need to deposit yesterday's dinner somewhere. The countryside is an ideal place for both, but responsible stewardship of the canine companion is still essential. Go for a walk along a quiet country track or area of woodland and within 100 yards of any car parking area it can feel like one has stumbled on a minefield. Dog faeces litters the path or verge, when either a doggy bag or a 'flick with a stick' into the bushes, would address the problem.

The following poem makes my point. Please feel free to reproduce it as you see fit.

Ode to a Dog Turd

Curling, steaming on the path,
May him on high throw down his wrath.
Go fetch a shovel. It is his bidding,
In case some walker should go skidding.

From whence you came you may not know.
Behind, above or from below.
But what is certain I can tell,
You're freshly ripened, by your smell.

Lingering long upon the grass,
Unless some responsible soul should pass
And take a bag to put you in,
Then deposit you inside a bin.

But, if none should find for thee a home,
You'll be here sitting on your own,
Unless some canine should along
And deliver up another one.

Upon your form dark flies will mass.
Some hundred eggs may come to pass.
Soon a writhing throng of gorging grubs.
Then a million flies within these woods.

All are welcome in this park.
A wildlife home, a Noah's Ark.
Old man hobbling, young child stalking,
Or even by chance with dog you're walking.

So, long it waits beside the path,
Waiting to have the last ones laugh.
Go fetch a shovel. It is our bidding,
In case it's you who does the skidding.

November 2017

The Commissioning Editor, rang me back within minutes of sending it, saying "Are you trying to kill me? We are a family paper. We can't publish 28 lines of poetry about dog mess".

I replied "My 85 year old mother-in-law thought it was hilarious, but it is not a problem. I'll be guided by you, as always. I'll send you an alternative article."

(Ironically this poem was the one I had sent with my initial Frontline News suggestion two years earlier, as an example of my work!)

******

Waiting to be Processed

Context:

November 2017's offering having been rejected, I quickly emailed this alternative:

Anyone who has sat in a GP's waiting room will probably have had a similar experience at some stage in their life.

Column:

I enter the GP waiting room and register my presence at reception, whilst a gentle piece of Schubert plays in the background. Suddenly a familiar Nokia ringtone blasts out across the room destroying the calm ambiance so carefully crafted by the great Austrian. I charitably assume that one of the waiting patients has accidentally forgotten to turn their mobile phone off. However, for the next 5 minutes we are entertained to the medical history of the lady's dog, which is currently at the vets. The receptionist looks irritated by the intrusion, but in typical English fashion says nothing. Others in the room twitch and sigh. To her credit the recipient of the call apologises meekly, as she sheepishly puts her mobile phone away.

With Schubert quickly hustled off the stage, Andreas Bocelli is wheeled on and attempts to restore calm with his gently soaring notes, as we all sit calmly awaiting our fate. Waiting rooms can feel a bit like abattoirs, in that we all sit patiently waiting to be processed by the professionals, as ignorant as pigs at the gates of a pork pie factory, or as a client of Sweeney Todd the Barber. In reality we are unlikely to end up in a pie, but our fears are nonetheless real, as we await the pronouncements of our GP.

No sooner has the Italian maestro finished and stands quietly in anticipation of applause, then yet another mobile goes off. You might expect 'callow youth' to be the least aware of protocols in a waiting room, but it is yet another lady of advancing years who is the culprit. As she puts the mobile to her ear "eine kleine nachtmusik" strikes up. This is going to be an uneven contest, with Mozart's strings standing no chance against 21st century communications technology. As if to rub the composer's nose in it, the culprit of the intrusion loudly issues an expletive. Yet again we sit listening to one-side of a conversation. Pursed lipped the receptionist glares in the direction of the miscreant, who shows no remorse for her indiscretions.

Before Wolfgang Amadeus' music has chance to restore my premedical contemplation, I am spared further mobile phone interruptions, as the nurse ushers me in for my blood test. The pork pie factory gates open wide as I enter the surgery. In a trice I am relieved of a worrying quantity of essential body fluids, before being efficiently sent packing in readiness for the next little pig. I am relieved to have escaped being turned into one of Mrs Lovett's pies, but considering how mysterious are the workings of the NHS and how strapped for cash they are, who is to say that at least some of me won't end up in one of her delicious black puddings?

November 2017

Alas, although presented for the November 2017 issue, it was never published. Someone forgot to tell me that my services were no longer required. That was until I bought a copy of the November issue, (yes I did have to buy my own!) only to find I was not there. When I queried this I got the following email response:

"...it turns out that the editor-in-chief got involved in the discussion of your column and felt that it didn't strike the right tone for us. One of my jobs was to let you know that the last one you'd contributed would be the last one we'd carry..."

Battle Frontline News – RIP

Frontline News Extra

The following is a short piece entered for the 950th celebrations of the Battle of Hastings in 2016. The brief was to write exactly 1066 words on a piece entitled "Battle 2066".

Battle 2066

I well recall 1966. It was the year we last won the World Cup and the year I bought my Battle of Hastings Commemorative stamps. To a 12 year old stamp collector they were absolutely fascinating. A strip of six 4d stamps, so long that you were pushed to find an envelope big enough to get the whole strip onto. Nonetheless, along with the 6d and 1s 3d stamps, they became the pride of my collection.

Then there was the 950th celebrations in 2016. Lot of fuss about nothing if you ask me. Someone was obviously looking for a reason to make a few bob, so they invented a special occasion. 1966, fair enough, that was a centenary and 2066 represents a whole millennium, but 950 years is neither one nor the other. Still English Heritage made a killing and most of the High Street traders as well. It was a good excuse for a party and to walk through the town in chain mail, with an arrow sticking out of your head. As usual the French came over in October, all dressed as Normans and the usual Saxon hordes were everywhere.

I remember when it all went wrong, during the re-enactment of the battle. Instead of singing the Song of Rollo, the French started chanting "Roast Beef Out", because the "Leave" campaign had won the referendum and we were no-longer in the EU. That got up the Saxon noses a bit, but it was the "We won the Cup" that really got their goat. For England to get all the way to the final of Euro 2016 only to be beaten by the French on penalties. It was just too much.

When the Normans did their usual faked retreat, the Saxons made their prescribed charge. Except on this occasion the Saxons refused to lie down dead. All hell broke out. Swords, shields, fists, spears, even frog's legs and a side of roast beef, were thrown. Bodies lay strewn all over the battlefield. Folks said it was the best they had ever seen and with the partisan crowd cheering them on, the Saxon's were declared the winners for the first time in 950 years. Cracking day. That was the last time that English Heritage hosted it. Prime Minister Farrage stood up in the house next day and declared England was great once again and demanded "William the Conqueror, who are you? And who voted for you?"

The French have blocked trade with Europe ever since. That's how we came to be part of the Indian Commonwealth with the Ghandi Dynasty as Heads of State. But then history often turns on a sixpence.

And so we come to 2066. At the grand old age of 112 I thought I had seen all that the Battle of Hastings can throw at us. For years arguments have been raging about where the battle actually took place. English Heritage of course refused to countenance any other site but the Abbey grounds, some guy in Crowhurst said it took place in his back yard, whilst Tony Robinson came out in favour of a mini-roundabout at the top of Marley Lane. Then in October, just as Battel Bonfire Boyes were about to begin their 50th battle re-enactment on The Recreation Ground, the news broke.

The new owners of the Calbec Hill windmill were getting their car park resurfaced, when the contractor's digger hit something solid and metallic. The county archaeologist was called in and a large lead coffin was extracted in front of hundreds of TV cameras and millions of viewers. Inside was the skeleton of a man bearing the signet ring of no less than Harold Godwinson. To cap it all he had been buried in his full armour, crown and all. Of course everyone started arguing about whether or not it was Harold of England's body or a fake. But when they carried out DNA tests they found a perfect match with a furniture maker in London, known to be related to Harold Godwinson's sister.

What really put the cat amongst the pigeons was Harold's eye. There was nothing wrong with it. Nothing wrong with either of them. Not an arrow in sight (literally). What is more there was not a wound on his body. Nothing.

So how had he died? Was it a bit of dodgy sea food from Hastings? Perhaps he had a sudden attack of syphilis contracted from Edith Swan-neck during his stopover in London, on the way back from Stamford Bridge. Or maybe the battle took so long to finish, that he just nodded off and someone presuming him dead, popped him into his 1000 year old casket.

Others want to know why he was buried on Calbec Hill? Was this the site of the Battle of Hastings? Perhaps his pall bearers were so knackered carrying his coffin up from Senlac Hill, that they popped him into the first convenient hole they came across. Maybe the foundations of a new windmill? Whatever, Battle

Observer were happy to sell a few more copies on the back of a good story. Of course the whole thing presented no surprise to most of us locals. Just about every other site in Battle had been investigated over the previous 50 years, as all the new housing estates, link roads and airport were built.

So there you have it. It all took place a thousand years ago on top of Calbec Hill. If William and Harold had come back to the site of their confrontation just 50 years ago, the view towards Netherfield would not have looked a great deal different from what it did in 1066. But 50 years on the place has changed out of all recognition. The tea shops have all been replaced by curry houses and not a single hairdressers is to be seen now that we all wear turbans. Perhaps the biggest change since 2016 is the demolition of Battle Abbey and the creation of the new Indian Heritage theme park. One thing that has not changed is the number of tourist shops on the High Street. The only change there is that they all now sell miniatures of the Taj Mahal.

Oh well, 112 years is quite long enough for one lifetime, same as the number of pounds in a hundred-weight. Still I suppose I can't complain, poor old Harold had a thousand year wait.

8/6/16

*****

Printed in Great Britain
by Amazon